MW00626018

Don't Let Your Struggles Separate You from God.

A Memoir and Real-Life Inspirational Poems

This book contains a memoir of real-life poems based on real-life experiences. From the depths of the authors heart, she tells and shares some of her struggles through her memoir and poems.

Copyright @ 2021 Kristle Shanell Publishing, LLC

All Rights Reserved.

No part of this publication may be reproduced in any form or by any means, electronic or mechanical, to

include photocopying, recording, or otherwise, without prior written permission from the publisher.

Printed in the United States Of America.

Inquiries should be addressed to as follows:

Kristle Shanell Publishing, LLC

Have you ever considered publishing a book??? Contact Us @

KristleShanellPublishing@gmail.com

ISBN: 978-1-7344874-04

The Struggle is Real; "But God!"

Memoir and Real-Life Inspirational Poems

"Yea, though I walk through the valley of the death, I will fear no evil; for thou art with me."
(Psalm 23:4, KJV)

Table of Contents

Dedication

I dedicate this book to my God, the Creator of Heaven and Earth, the Author and Finisher of my Faith. I thank him for the inspiration and the encouragement he gave to me to write this book.

To my husband of over 45 years, thank you. To my precious children: Wesley, Danisha, and Kristle. To my wonderful grandchildren, you are the joy of my life.

To my beloved father and mother, the late James and Ida Brown, who through the struggles, still kept the family together. To my brothers and sisters, especially (my eldest brother and sister) James Brown and Genetta Brown Brunson, who at an early age left the South and moved to New York to help provide for the family. Oh, how I appreciate you.

To my dear friend, who encourages and holds me dear through the good and bad times. To my church family who was a great support to me. A special thanks to my baby daughter, Kristle, who has encouraged and inspired me through the writing of this book; thank you baby girl.

To my nieces and nephews who have always been there for me.

Foreword

I was first introduced to the writings of Rachel Jenkins when I visited her in her native land of South Carolina. We were sitting in her living room, talking about the Lord (something she does all the time) and she shared that she had written a poem. She then proceeded to read it to me. I was impressed and at the same time amazed at how God gives His people so much talent and creative abilities. Silly me thought this was the only poem until she declared that she had forty of them. She poetically invites us along her journey through a life of faith and trust in God. Rachel's poems are her sharing God's light with a world that can sometimes be so dark. As you read these offerings you will see that in her life God is Savior, Healer, Protector and Father. Rachel encourages us to remember God in the midst of our struggles. He's with you when they come, He's with you as you go through, He's with you when they end.

Read on my friend and let these utterings from her heart bless your heart.

Carolyn Shumate
Playwright, Poet

A Prayer for the Readers from the Author

Father God in the name of Jesus, you are good, your awesomeness is above all others. I thank you oh God for life, health, and strength. Lord every morning with you I am renewed. I praise and magnify your Holy and Righteous Name. I exalt you oh God, for there is done like you. You are the only true and wise God.

God I'm asking that you bless every reader that read this book of poems that was given by your inspiration. Let the words on these pages prick the hearts of every reader Lord, as I share these real-life experiences, allow it to witness to others the Awesomeness of your Spirit. Lord, I thank you for the Power you have given unto me.

Lord I dedicated this book to you. My prayer is that this book will encourage, inspire, and cause others to put their truth in you. In Jesus name Amen.

A Special Testimony

My Mission: is to reach the lost and the broken hearted. To serve those in need, encourage the Saints of the Most High God; while I joyfully take my quest through our Global and Diverse Society.

"I will bless the Lord at all times and his praise shall continually be in my mouth."

In spite of all the conflicts, wars, and our unpredictable economy, my soul makes her boast in the Lord. *"The Just shall live by Faith"*. Yes, the Just shall live by Faith, so encourage my soul and let us journey on.

As a woman of God, I have encountered many challenges. Some came to test me and there were others that came to shut me down, **"But GOD"**! By his grace I have overcame. I thank God I am still saved and filled with his Precious Holy Ghost.

"Many are called but few are chosen", oh how marvelous is the work and love of God. About age ten I was ran over by a farm truck while riding on the back of the tailgate of that truck. My foot hit the pavement and it drugged me under the truck I was riding on. The driver decided he would back up the truck to the farm where we were living at that time while working on the Tobacco Farm in North Carolina. There were other children on the truck at the time of the accident, but they did not get injured. I realized I could have gotten crushed, **but God!** He spared my life, and I am so grateful. I spent an extended amount time in the hospital, I suffered great scars, wounds, a broken leg and hip that left me in a body cast **but Lord I am still** GRATEFUL, because my scars were so severe, I refused to wear dresses or skirts in shame and fear someone would tease me of my ugly scared up legs. God has taken most of my scars away but left enough as a reminder to let me know.

I am still here because of Gods Great LOVE for me. He has chosen me today to share this Testimony with you.

I accepted Jesus as my Personal Savior at age nineteen and he has been my all and all. He has done great and Marvelous things in my life, and Lord I am GRATEFUL. I encourage those that are filled with the Holy Ghost, let us continue to live for the Lord in the Beauty of Holiness.

My Brothers and my Sisters I know the journey is sometimes rough and rugged, but remember we are not walking alone. Jesus is right there carrying us along so be encouraged.

And for those that have not accepted Jesus as your personal Savior, please.

"Repent, and be baptized, every one of you in the name of Jesus Christ for the remission of sins, and ye shall receive the gift of the Holy Ghost."

Acts 2: 38

About The Author

Thank you, God for my father and mother
About them I will go no further
The eighth of wonderful nine
It's alright, I don't mind.

Life was tough and we did not have much,
Family back then kept in touch
Through grade school and middle school too
In High school I meet you know who!

Start dating at an early age, and this is what went wrong,
Got pregnant with a little boy oh so young.
He was handsome my pride and joy
Many times, no money to buy him a toy.

Married my "High School Sweetheart" you see
We was happy as we could be
Five years later I pray for a little girl
She came, and it change my world!

A boy and a girl this was sweet
A constant reminder that I kept them in the heat
Moma's little boy and daddy's little girl, they would say
At an early age, oh how I learned to pray!

Five years later, God shifted our plan
Didn't bother me much, my husband was a working man
Another little girl came in December
The Joy she brought to the family; I remember!

Early Satan start making his attacks!
With the word of God, I kept fighting back
A young grandmother I became
TJ, some call him, but Torrence was his name

Oh, the happiness and joy my grandson brought!
A powerful lesson from God to me was taught
The grandchildren kept coming, now there are seven!
One great grandson God sent from Heaven

Satan still fighting and making his attacks
With the word of God, I am still fighting back!
I pray these poems will help along the way
Hope it will lift your spirits and encourage you each day
"The Struggle is real" I heard someone say
I ask for his strength each day as I pray!

"I will bless the Lord at all time His praise shall continually be in my mouth"

Psalm 34:1

Testimonial and Memoir

Chapter One

Inspired

Most of my life I experienced tremendous rejections and negative challenges that consumed me. These experiences threatened to keep me from who and what God has called me to do. Especially when it comes to using my purpose and destiny in the Kingdom of God. As a young black girl from the South, and a family of nine siblings in which only two graduated high school, the odds were against me. I was one of two of my parents' children to graduate high school. I went even further and graduated from college. Although, I did not get the career that I pursued in college, I remain faithful in my present job.

I went to work faithfully every day as a school Bus Driver, a Substitute Teacher, and later a Teacher's Assistance. Although I was rejected and disrespected by the students many times, I would still perform at my best and share the love God imparted in me. It seemed like every negative thing that was done to me, God would allow me to turn it into a revelation as to how He wanted me to make it into something positive. The words that would run through my head would be from God's Word; the spirit would let me know this: If they did it to Jesus, they will do it to you.

I knew early in life I wanted to write a book and tell my story, but the enemy would try to influence my intension. What the enemy wanted me to write was not the type of book I wanted to write. What I have written is how I was inspired by the Holy Spirit. I picked up my pen one day and wrote a poem from the very depth of my heart and from effort, the Spirit took over. I was inspired to write these poems and tell my life stories through them.

My inspiration for writing this book came from God. There were those who imparted in me how to stand tall and pursue my dreams. I would say my mother inspired me. She was a woman that couldn't read or write, but she took what she had and used it to her full potential. She used her hands to help provide and care for her husband and nine children. She would also sew our clothes, chair coverings, and table coverings (just to name a few of the many items that she sewed with her hands).

Rev. James Glover Jr., a former pastor that I loved so dearly, helped in preparing my Christian walk. Bishop Joe and Mother Barbra Brooks were the two people that molded me after God's own way. Preaching and teaching me "in season and out of season", the profound word of God. They instilled into me a more perfect way. I thank God for them.

There are still those Fathers and Mothers of the Church of Our Lord Jesus Christ; all stood as pillars and role models to me.

Oprah Winfrey, has and still is a great inspiration to me in my life struggles. She has impacted me in great ways. I love her strength, drive, and perseverance. I subscribed to her magazine, watched her TV Shows, and always wanted to meet her in person. I am a saved black woman and I know God is not through with me; He favors me. I know that I am a chosen vessel.

Lastly, my beloved Chief Apostle William L. Bonner's powerful preaching and teaching transformed my life. When I first came into the Church of Our Lord Jesus Christ, I met a giant man of God. He was a giant yet humble as a lamb. He had love for everyone. His faith was immeasurable. After reading his book "Positive Thinking Changed My Life," my life has never been the same. What a great inspiration he has been to me.

Chapter Two

Just Do It

With all the challenges and odds that came to engulf my thoughts, a voice within me said "Just Do It." I picked up my pen and began to write. "You can do this," the voice said, "Oh, yes you can." I began my path that I so long wanted to pursue, and that is to tell my story in hopes that I may encourage someone along the way.

When you are challenged by the cares and trials of this life, don't let it stop you from pursuing your dreams. It has been said that your struggles sometimes come to *make* you. When going through the birthing period, it is sometimes real hard. It is not always easy, but if you can endure, what you deliver will be something beautiful in the Kingdom of God. Don't let fear hold you back, "Just Do It."

When I began to write, I realized that writing can be unpredictable, especially if you are being guided by the Holy Spirit. When He speaks, you write, sometimes it can be in the morning hours, the midday, in the evening time, or even in the midnight hours. Many times, I had to get out of bed and began to write. You just have to do it. The poems would just come to me.

I could have written many more poems but was inspired to stop at number 40. I thank God for the vision.

Sometimes you just have to encourage yourself. Don't let anything or anyone overshadow your dream.

"Fret not thyself because of evildoers, neither be thou envious against the workers of iniquity. For they shall soon be cut down like the grass, and wither as the green herb. Trust in the Lord and DO GOOD; verily thou shalt be fed. Delight thyself in the Lord and he shall give thee the desires of thine heart."

Psalm 37: 1-4

Chapter Three

The Struggles

Struggle is not a modern-day term. It has been around for a very long time. It was here when I was born, for some it will be here when Jesus makes His return. The struggle is real. There are different struggles. Struggles can sometimes make people stronger. It can sometimes cause others to give up, but don't let it cause you to give up on God or your life's dreams.

I have come through many struggles that robbed me and also held me captive. I am from an ANGER family of nine siblings. Only two of us graduated from high school and I am only one to graduate from college.

Living in the South was not easy for us. We did not have much. I stayed out of school equal to the time of me going to school. We had to go in the fields to pick beans, cucumbers, cotton, pick up pecans, rake yards, etc. It was a must that we stay home from school to work for our landlords. Whatever the people we worked for wanted us to do, we did it. Sometimes it would be picking up pecans. At other times, we would be cleaning chickens, raking yards, or killing and preparing hogs.

My sisters and brothers would work hard each day. Many times, our pay would be some year-before pecans, chicken feet, or hog guts (a term we would use for hog intestines). This would be the pay they would give us for our labor. We would thank God, because sometimes this would be all that we had. Our parents told us that their parents taught them never to say "No" to the white man." They said, "even if we don't want their stuff, just take it".

The struggles were real; this was the reality for me and my family. As I stated before, we did not have much, but our love kept the family together. Going from one "white-owned" farm to another was the pattern my dad set for us children.

We had no electricity or running water at home. Sometimes we had to go and gather water from a distance. My siblings and I had to go into the woods to gather firewood to burn to keep us warm.

As a young child, I just could not understand the lesson my parents taught us about never saying "No" to the "white man," even if you don't want their stuff; my parents always told us to just take it."

Well, as I began to grow older, I became more knowledgeable that we were yet going through some form of slavery, working for a little of nothing, and not having the right to freedom of speech. The boldness to speak began to rise in me. I can remember it so well, as if it happened yesterday. I told my mom boldly that if Mr. Haynes would bring any more of those hog guts to our house, I was going to tell him to take it back because we don't want them.

As I stated, hog guts were a term we used for hog intestines. My mom would receive the hog guts, and then we had to bury them. Well, I just got tired of the stinky stuff and was about to make an attempt to put it to an end. I wanted them to keep their stinky stuff and do whatever they wanted to do with them. Well, an angel must have visited with Mr. Haynes because he never brought any more. I was now ready to change the term from "Don't say no" to "Yes, we can."

"If it had not been for the Lord who was on our side."

Psalm 124

Chapter Four

The Hurt, Shame & Struggles

any hurts and shame over the years deeply affected my life, beginning with my childhood. We ere very poor, and poverty brought shame and hurt to me.

y brothers, sisters, and I experienced the racism that was part of the times in which we were orn and brought up. My siblings and I were teased and rejected by many. Sometimes even mily members, but love kept us together. We were constantly reminded that we were not ntitled to the same rights that white people were born into, and that being a person of color as not something of which we should be proud. Even my last name (Brown) when I was a child, emed to have a reproach on me.

eing young and hearing so many negative things about the Browns led me to feel some-what hamed to embrace my roots. As I grew older and accepting Jesus as my personal savior, I ank God for my family ties. I came to realize that my family, (the Brown family) has a rich eritage, to God be the Glory!

ne enemy came to "kill, steal and destroy", but God brought us over. I feel blessed now that I n share a little of what my life was like growing up.

either my mom nor dad could read and write. The both of them work endlessly to provide for e family. My oldest brother James and oldest sister Genetta left the south for New York at an arly age to take on the great responsibility of helping provide for the family. They worked and nt money and clothes down South for us. They would come home and visit sometimes during olidays. We would be so glad to see them and sad when they would go back. We would cry orely when it was time for them to leave and return to New York.

e did not have much, but mom was oh so clean. She made sure that her children were kept ean too. She would make us take off our clothes after school and would wash them for us to ut on the following day. Having no sewing machine in the home, mom would make things for s by hand, such as undergarments as well as dresses and skirts, etc. She did all of this by hand.

y dad would drink and get drunk (this also brought hurt and shame on me). He would get runk, come home, and get into fights with my mom. My mom was a good fighter, so she would y to defend herself. It really hurt me to witness this kind of behavior from my parents, but rough the hurts and shame God brought me through.

My desire today is, **God teach them to love the one they say they love.** I would ask myself many times whether these are trials I am supposed to bear as a good soldier, and if I endure, have I passed the test?

It would come to mind that I should endure hardship as a good soldier. Does the Word of God mean we must take all the blows and then we have passed the "Test of Trials?"

I would make excuses for the behaviors and took the good and the bad. I would say the good outweighed the bad. I know "the enemy comes to steal, kill and destroy", and he does this well, but I won't let him do what he came to do.

Writing this book is one of the tools I decided to use to try and help encourage any individual

out there with a problem to seek help and be on the road to recovery. The individual *must* adm there is a problem; this is the first step. Just like when we were sinners and wanted to become saved, we had to first confess we were a sinner; then Jesus Christ stood with His arms open to save us. He is still standing with his arms open to help us.

Through the struggles I can still see the good, but how good is good when you are in pain at the time. When we don't fix the problem that is at hand; this can be handed down from generation to generation. It will grow bigger unless someone steps up and leads a change.

In our society today, many lives are being lost through abuse and domestic violence. The divorce rate is still far too high. There are problems deeper than some are willing to accept. I believe out there in society are men and women with undiagnosed behavior and we continue to accept the fact the individual will change. Many times things get worst instead of better. When I was growing up, mental Illness was something we were ashamed of. People did not even call it mental Illness. People would say the individual was losing his or her mind or the individual was crazy. This would bring shame on a family, but today there are resources to help that one that is struggling with mental illness.

Sisters and brothers let us not sit back and be content; let us continue to love but in loving, let us help to bring about a change. Too many of our brothers and sisters are being killed and the others are being hauled to jail. We know when the head is fixed, the body will stay connected.

"And it shall come to pass, if thou shalt hearken diligently unto the voice of the Lord thy God, to observe and to do all his commandments which I command thee this day, that the Lord thy God will set thee on high above all nations of the earth. And all these blessings shall come on thee, and overtake thee. Blessed shall thou be when thou comest in and blessed shall thou be when thou goest out."

Deuteronomy 28:

Chapter Five

Deliverance

"I come to give you life and that more abundantly," says our God. Satan's attacks came to take me back into bondage, but the Holy Spirit did not let them. I fuel my life daily with the Word of God. *"Greater is He that is in me than he that is in the world". "I can do all things through Christ which strengthen me."*

I am no longer bound; I have been delivered; I have been set free. I can see more clearly now. When Satan makes his attacks, they don't overtake me, the Blood of Jesus shelters me in from his many snares. His protection was always true, even when I was raising my children and even during a career in which I was teaching other people's children.

Being in the educational arena taught me many things. It taught me patience, perseverance, and so much more. I was privileged to see my purpose in the Kingdom of God. Being a school bus driver and an instructional teacher's aide, I was confronted with many challenges.

Disrespect seems to have been a daily occurrence, but I still loved the children God entrusted me to teach. I learned how to give all the situations that came to engulf me to Jesus. I always leaned on Him because I knew He is the rock of my salvation.

Even through the educational arena has been a challenge, it has afforded me many opportunities; I enjoy what I did, and working as a team to help the betterment of our dear students helped me to learn that children are gifts sent from God. All are unique in their own way. A little love and concern sometimes helps to open up the way to a positive beginning.

Since God delivered me, I learned how to press forward to my destiny. Destiny is always in front of you and not behind. No matter the attack or attacks the enemy may bring in your home, your marriage, against your loved ones, or even in your place of employment stay strong and be encouraged. Through my deliverances, I have been inspired to write this book, not with enticing words I come, but from my heart, I share this with you.

What is deliverance, some may ask? Let me share the definition with you. According to Webster's Dictionary, Deliver means *"to set free, save; to hand over, recue, to produce the promised desired; or expected results."*

My concept of deliverance is, *"one day I was lost, but now I am found, I was blind but now I see".* Jesus Christ came and rescued me; He set me free.

Yes, at an early age I surrendered my life to Christ, and He delivered me from all the guilt and shame that covered me for years. I repented of my sins and Jesus opened His loving arms and received me with His love. I no longer hold my head down in shame, I have been delivered.

When the hurt comes, I know how to turn it over to Jesus. Gods word told us to "cast all our cares upon Him for He cares for us". I am delivered and now I know for sure who I am. I am a child of the Most High God, and I put a praise on that. My walk has been changed, my talk has changed, my desires have changed, and my life is no longer the same. When I look back over my life I can truly say, it was the Lord that brought me through.

I can say that since I got delivered every day is not sunshine, but the difference now is, I got Jesus and He is able.

"For God so loved the world that he gave His only begotten Son that whosoever believeth in Him should not perish, but have everlasting life."

John 3: 16

Life Inspired Poems

Why 40?

The following pages are 40 simple inspirational poems translated from real-life experiences, telling and sharing some of my life struggles, joys and fulfillments.

Writing these poems really detoxified my mind while refreshing the soul. My desires are that the poems will bless someone and encourage them to know that no matter what the struggle(s) may be, never give up on God. We are our Father's children, and He knows each one of our names. He sees and knows the struggles that we have to bear.

I wanted to keep writing but the number 40 was given to me as a hallmark ending. The number 40 is a very *significant number in the Bible.*

Forty: The Number of Testing

*Forty days Jesus was tempted by the devil in the wilderness. Matthew 4:1
*And the Lord said to Moses, write these words for in accordance with these words I have made a Covenant with the Lord forty days and forty nights. He neither ate, bread nor drink water. And he wrote on the tablets the words of the Covenant, the "Ten Commandments." Exodus 34:27-28

*For the people of Israel walked forty years in the wilderness, until all the nation, the men of war who came out of Egypt, perished, because they did not obey the voice of the Lord, the Lord swore to them that He would not let them see the land that the Lord had sworn to their Fathers to give to us, a land flowing with milk and honey. Joshua 5:6
*And the Rain fell upon the earth 40 days and 40 nights. Genesis 7:12
*Moses sent spies into the Promised Land and they were there 40 days and 40 nights before returning to give their report about the land. Numbers 13:25
*When Israel disobeyed, He gave them over to their enemies Forty years. Judges 13:1
*Isaac and Jacob were both 40 years old when they married.

But Still I Love

(Young, Married and Unaccepted)

Away from home in an unfamiliar town\
BUT STILL, I LOVE!
This man I adored, occupied with mama demand you see
No time for himself or for me
BUT STILL, I LOVE!

Under the same roof we did dwell
In a house with someone full of hell
Young and confused, this was me
The man I love is not able to see
BUT STILL, I LOVE!

Is something wrong, and I can't be?
Wanted to be accepted, was my only plea
Crossing each other path, felt like electricity
Hoping things would be better and his Mama would see
BUT STILL, I LOVE!

Kept apart day and night
God knows this isn't right
Together in his arms he did plan
Climb the stairs my love, yes you can
BUT STILL, I LOVE!

Up the stairs to meet my love
Young and afraid, wish I was a dove
In his arms, oh, at last
Trying to forget all the evil past
BUT STILL, I LOVE!

I was married but could not tell
We both kept it a secret in our hearts it dwelled
So afraid mama would know about this
Could not even give my husband a kiss
BUT STILL, I LOVE!

Can't Even Imagine

A poem written November 2015 for my nephew Derick

Woke up early this morning, my mind was on you
House a little chilly you see
But that's alright, had to get this out of me
God made family to be together
Loving, sharing, and taking care of each other
Through the sunshine and stormy weather
Our love always kept us together

Can't even imagine what it would be
If we could not share our love so free
The last past months God showed His best
He spared my sister, your aunt, and did not put her to rest

Life is just a vapor in the air
Must let family know we care
Can't even imagine what your grandmother so dear,
In so many words told me to keep the family in prayer
I am always here when family needs me
Lord keep us together, is my only plea

Which you were here but not meant to be
Down in our heart we hold you dearly
Can't even imagine life without family I must say
Pray for you both night and day

Closing this poem with a sweet, sweet ending
Now I feel free, like a dove ascending
Can't even imagine not having you
Don't have a single clue
I can't even imagine

Brokenness

Brokenness wanted to destroy the inner part of me
Came rushing like an untamed sea
The gulf opened its mouth to swallow me up
I cried; Lord please, please move this bitter cup

Sometimes it was like His spirit wasn't there
Kept talking to him in daily prayer
There were days when I felt so strong
Then the brokenness came and tried to push me down

Brokenness brings seeds of separation
Sudden decisions are made under desperation
Brokenness is not a friend to anyone
With the fight of faith, I have come

Brokenness is like a seed of sin
But with Christ Jesus we can win
Forgiveness will free all man
It's not easy but, *yes, we can*

Don't let brokenness bring you down
Be positive, be happy, and wear your crown
Brokenness comes to make you quit
But it won't win, not even a little bit

"Let not you heart be trouble: ye believe in God, believe also in me."

John: 14:1

Bridge Over Troubled Water

Bridge over troubled water, a pathway through life
Holding up every conflict and every strife
Embracing every diversity, great and small
A foundation not built by man, neither anchor in the soil

Bridge over troubled water, is it from above?
Holding strong it's unfailing love
Deep, deep and never sinking under
Bridge over troubled water I still do ponder

Bridge over troubled water, that open door that was shut
A foundation of joy that joyfully heals and not cut
How beautiful is thy strength and mite
Taking the storm and awaken the light

Bridge over troubled water helps fear to depart
Repairs the damage, that ravish the heart
Release from bondage shining as silver and gold
Bridge over trouble water refresh and lift up the soul

Bridge over trouble water a pathway through life
Holding up every conflict and every strife
Standing deep through the evening tides
Embracing every diversity from every side

"Blessed is the man that walketh not in the counsel of the ungodly, nor standeth in the way of sinners, nor sitteth in the seat of the scornful. But his delight is in the law of the Lord: and in His law doth meditate day and night. And he shall be like a tree planted by the rivers of water; that bringeth forth his fruit in his season."

Psalm 1:1-3

Black

Black is beautiful, this I know
Told myself and this, I am sure
Look in the mirror and what do I see
A black woman beautiful and pretty as she can be

Black is a color that not easily changed to another
The black skin has shades that can embrace many types of weather
Black was there from the beginning of time
You will find this in the bible timeline

Black is a color that is sometimes rejected
Black is a color that many times is not respected
Black was the color our ancestors, some lost their lives
Black was the color that brought them so much hate, envy and strife

Black was the color why she could not sit on the front of the bus
Black is the color when we stand together, they afraid of us
Black was the color; the white men took their wives
Black was the color so many black men lost their lives

Black is like the midnight sky
For our rights many have surely died
Black is the color that was looked down upon
Hand in hand, many battles they have won

Black is beautiful, this I know
Told myself and this, I am sure
Black was here from the beginning of time
You will find this all through the Biblical timeline

"In the beginning God created the heaven and earth. And God said, Let us make man in our image, in the image of God created him; male and female created them."

Genesis: 1: 1 -1: 26-27

I Believe

I believe in Christ and all His glory
I believe in all His words totally
I believe he died for everyone
I believe God and Christ are one

I believe He bleed, suffered and died
I believe He did it for your sins and mine
I believe the grave could not hold his body down
I believe at the cross they treated him wrong

I believe He had power over the grave
I believe by this, we were saved
I believe with His strips we are healed
I believe our victory; Satan wants to steal

I believe we can speak His words
I believe His words must be heard
I believe He is the True Vine
I believe joy in Him we will find

I believe In Christ and all His glory
I believe in His word totally
I believe, I believe

"I am the true vine, and my Father is the husbandman. As the Father has love me, so have I loved you; continue in my love."

John: 15: 1, 9

Anger

The toxicity that controls and changes and don't care who
Takes over and can destroy you, too
Saw the monster with the naked eye
Wanted to understand, I would ask why?

Anger comes charging even in the break of day
Cries out; Lord, I don't know what to say
Oh, the gloom that takes its joy
Like a little boy losing a special toy

Search to see what is done wrong
Sometimes it helps to sing a song
Anger can travel even on the freeway
Anger can set everything at bay

Can't stop anger when it's in rage
You are not on the same page
Let anger take it coast until it cools off
Then approach it again, talking very soft

Anger can root up the deepest love
Even love that were cultivated like a bud
Let anger take its coast and let it be known
Before long it will find it's all alone

"No weapon that formed against thee shall prosper; and every tongue that shall rise against thee in judgment thou shall condemn."

Isaiah 54:17

A Virtuous Wife

(Wives, Love Your Husband)

She trusts in him and can feel his love and care
She will do him good and not evil
The love they share is unbelievable
She riseth also while it is night
To see if her children and true love are alright

She will stretch out her hands to help the poor
She will stretch out her hand to help the needy
She is not worried of what tomorrow will bring
A song in her heart she always hummed and sing

Her husband's name she tries to protect
She opens her mouth with wisdom and respect
Never on her face will she wear a frown
She speaks well of her husband all over town

A Virtuous Woman God called her to be
Even when her husband is not willing to see
My precious love you are to me
I am your wife and I praise God for thee

"Who can find a Virtuous Woman? For her price is far above rubies."

Proverb: 31:10

A Change Will Come

Speak the word and a change will come
I am a witness that it has already happened for some
Speak the word and believe what you have said
Speak it as if it was your daily bread

A change will come if you would believe
Open your heart and you can receive
Don't let the enemy bring you doubt
That is what his tricks are all about

A change will come if you stay with God's Word
Many wonderful testimonies I have heard
A change will come and this I know
It will come just like an open door
A change will come sometime overnight
Sometimes it seems like a change isn't in sight
Just one change may be the request
As you go through your many tests

"He shall call upon me, and I will answer him: I will be with him in trouble; I will deliver Him, and I will honor him."

Psalm: 91: 15

Christmas Memory

Not so very long ago, being a child, I did not know
Oh, what Christmas meant, you see
Focus was on the presents under the tree

The gifts we got seem so very cute
Was told it came from Santa, the man in the red suit
Mom and dad worked hard to give to us all,
but the credit went to the man in the red suit; that stands in store malls

Mom and them did not tell us about Jesus birth
Busy getting our food from the earth
Us children would search for a pine tree
Back at the house was the smell of cornbread
And that good old sweet, sweet, tea

Mom and them did not tell us about Jesus's birth
But made sure we knew what those gifts were worth
Mom and Dad work from sunup to sundown
Still no car, they had to walk all the way to town

We did not know Christmas was about Jesus's birth
But the love we shared valued more than mirth
Now, I know what Christ means
In my life Christ will forever be seen

So many debates about Jesus's birth I've got
Should we celebrate or should we not
Silent night is one of the Christmas tone
My belief is that Christ is coming back soon

Matthew 1:18-25, 2:1-2

Come To Jesus

Have you heard of the Redemption Story?
To Him belongs all the glory
Accept Jesus in your heart today
Jesus is truly the only way

God so loved the world; He gave His only begotten son
To Jesus you can freely run
Love Him with all of your might
Do the things that you know are right

If you are lost, He can turn you around
In Jesus you will be safe and sound
With Christ, there is joy peace and freedom
Living and working in His daily Kingdom

Come to Jesus and do it today
The love you feel, you want to stay
He is standing with his arms open wide
Patiently waiting to free you from the devil side

Come to Jesus today

*"For God so loved the world, that He gave his only begotten son, that whosoever
Believeth in him should not perish but have everlasting life."*

John: 3: 16

3

Expecting The Expected

I expected love to be sweet, gentle and caring
Not hard, cold, brutal and unbarring
I expected love to hold me up when I am down
Not withdrawn, apart and embracing me with a frown

I expected love to understand when I am in pain
Not crush me and make me feel like a victim on a chain
I expected love to be there when I need it the most
Not so far away, is it there; or is it a ghost?

I expected love to share in my trouble
Not make things worse or double
I expected love to say I care
Not leave it all for me to bear

I expected love to reach out its arm
Not seeing the hurt and still sit so calm
I expected love to reach out to me
Not leave and go like you don't see

I expected love to let me know I am adored
Not make me cry until I am sore
I expected love to hold me when things are not right
My love my love let me know you are somewhere in sight

"And we know that all things work together for good to them that love God, to them who are
the called according to his purpose."

Roman 8:28

Faith

(It was faith, it took faith, to bring me through my Wilderness Experience...Cancer)

It was faith, Abraham and Sarah waited for a son
It took faith, when Joseph was sold by his brothers
It was faith, Noah built an Ark when he was told
It took faith, Jacob wrestled with the angel until the morning came

It was faith, when Moses answered to his call
It took faith for David to defeat Goliath
It was faith when Samuel defeated the Palestine
It took faith, Hanna prayed for a child

It was faith, Elijah prayed for rain
It took faith for them to cross the red sea
It was faith, Ruth entered a strange land
It took faith, Ester went in to see the king

It was faith, Enoch was baptized
It took faith, Paul and Silas when in jail sang and prayed
It was faith, the woman with the issue of blood, touched the hem of His garment
It took faith for the three Hebrew boys in the fire of the furnace

It was faith, Daniel being in the lion's den
It took faith for Peter to walk on water
It was faith, the blind man received his sight
It took faith, Zaris' daughter was raised from the dead
It was faith, yes, it took faith

"Now faith is the substance of things hoped for, the evidence of things not seen."
Hebrews 11:1

Friend

I call you friend and not a Servant
The words Jesus spoke to His disciples
A friend will be there in the good times and the bad
Knows when you are down or when you are sad

A friend, a friend, oh, how I treasure her love
Can't remember when we met, but it was from above
From that day, oh, the joy we shared
It's in our hearts, it follows us everywhere

The word of God we shared when we often talk
She is a dear friend, very active, and loves to walk
A friend that helps and a friend that supports
Always positive when confronted with challenging reports

A friend who drinks with you from your bitter cup
A friend who will be there when you say you had enough
God give us friends to be there when we are alone
Some was given before we were born

A friend who cries and laughs with you too
Someone you can depend on; this I really knew
These are words from a friend's mouth
About two friends from way down South

Can't let conflicts tear us apart
What we share is from the heart
Be a friend, you will have a friend, you will see
A friend is good to have, I know you will agree

"A friend loveth at all times."

Proverb 17:17

Happy Birthday

Got up feeling very good
Getting ready as fast as I could
Joy and gratefulness grace the air
It's my Birthday what should I wear

In my heart I believe he cares
His silence is sometimes a bit much to bear
Calls coming, but I really have to go
Making my way to the door

Texts after texts, I saw the phone lit up
Trying to be strong, as I drink from this cup
I must go and get things done
Time is moving, can almost see the morning sun

Thank God, he gave me another birthday
My Love, for my True Love, I often pray
Birthdays come every year to us
Celebrating each other, this should be a must

Fight really hard so our love won't grow dim
Doing all the things I promise to do for him
More birthdays behind me than in front of me
Bless with another birthday was the key

My birthday it did go well
Not too many people I did tell
When someone you love finally say,
I love you my dear, would be the best birthday

"Bless the Lord O my soul: and all that is within me bless his holy name."

Psalm: 103:1

How Could You?

Woman with children down in the Deep South
Cruel things about her children often came from her mouth
I got to meet her at a young age, many years ago
Many things about her I did not know

How could you have a child who almost died?
Did not respond in any way, we often asked why?
One of her sons was very special to me
Things we did not understand, we let it be

How could you not have been there at our marriage celebration?
So far away when we went through great temptation
You were not there when the grandchild was born
He was a blessing, not someone to be scorned

How could you not tell, that so many times we needed you
It broke our heart because showing love was all we would do
Not a kind word you would say about some
Did not want to hear it, but we would continue to come

How could you not want us to come and pray?
In rage and anger you wanted to hurt me the next day
One of her sons was very special to me
Things in his past I believe holds the key

How could you when you were growing old
Could not embrace your love ones but stayed so cold
It broke our hearts because showing love was all we would do
We hoped and prayed that you knew we really loved you

Waited

Oh, how I waited for just a touch
To me, this would mean so much
Thoughts running through my head
Sitting here on side of my bed

The enemy will rob, steal and kill
Especially being in God's holy will
The hurt and pain I did feel
Love must be share or the enemy will steal

Oh, how I waited for just one touch
To me, this would mean so much
The hurt, the pain I know he feels
My love, his heart I want let the enemy steal

No longer two, but the two become one
In my thoughts and heart, this I would pond
Love isn't cold nor is it dim
His love for me and my love for him

You know me God, you know me well
Your power has kept me, this I can tell
Lord don't leave me; let me feel your loving touch
Keep reminding me you love me, oh so much

"Wait on the Lord: be of good courage, and he shall strengthen thine heart: Wait I Say, on the Lord."

Psalm: 27:14

In the Stillness of the Night

What do I see and what do I hear?
Sometimes joy but mostly loneliness I'll bear
Lying here hoping it would be
The empty nothing controlling the atmosphere
In the stillness of the night

Someone is here next to me
Darkness stretches its arms in despaired
Thousands of things going through my head
Are these afflictions I'm supposed to bear?
Can't explain, can't explain, I tell myself
In the stillness of the night

Shut up in this dark cage in the middle of nowhere
Questioning my questions, trying to make sense
Awake, asleep, and then up again
Searching through this darkness thick as brick
Can't make sense of it, in the stillness of the night

Daybreak, springtime, sunshine and then winter comes all over again
Mind racing around every channel it can
Tears pour from the fountain built up for years
Will not let it engulf a power so strong
In the stillness of the night

Pathway out of the darkness I tried to climb
Unlocking the gate trying to be free
Never coming back in this place, never again
The anointing flowing over me is real
Daybreak is seen, in the stillness of the night

"Yea, though I walk the valley of the shadow of death, I will fear no evil: for thou art with."
Psalm 23:4

Life

Created by the Hands of God through creation
A world that was void and no foundation
Man was created from the dust, then came life
It all started from Adam and his wife

Life has its ups and has its downs
A creation where nothing God made was wrong
Man was made in God's own image you see
Is this the reason Satan fights you and me?

Life is too precious to allow the loss of one
Fathers, mothers, daughters, and yes, our sons
Life was what God predestined for all
The devil came with his trickery, man did fall

Out of the garden man was driven
But He gave His son, and our sins can be forgiven
Why die when you can live forever
Pain, heartaches, and sickness these things will be, never

A place Christ has gone to prepare for us
For every believer, even our loved ones we already placed in the dust
Life is what God predestined for all
A plan was given even after man fall

Live life to the fullest day by day
Remember your sisters and brothers when you pray
Life is not how you take it
But life is what you make it

"In the beginning God created the heaven and the earth."

Genesis 1:1

"And the Lord God formed man of the dust of the ground, and breathed into his nostrils the breath of life; and man became a living soul."

Genesis 2:7

Lost Hair

The hair was given to women for her glory
My lost hair left me to tell this story
I look in the mirror with my eyes I do stare
Losing my hair, oh, Lord it just don't seem fair

The whole head it is all so bare
Talk to myself and then whisper a prayer
Nothing wrong with wearing it bald, said some
Maybe the day I wear it bald will come

Look at my baldness and sometimes I want to cry
I turn to God, and many times I ask God, why
This bald head tries to rob me,
but I hold fast to my integrity

A constant wound that wants to bother me
In my mirror, amazed at what I see
Long, black and coarse hair, once covered my head
Refuse to except my roots are dead

The hair was given to women for her glory
Lost hair left me to tell this story
Hair is not what makes you
Your spirit and personality do

Don't judge one with head covering
Lost hair could be the thing she is suffering
See the person and not her hair
Under the covering is one so dear

Don't ask, is that your hair?
See the person and feel her care
Never mind if the hair is black or tan
Under the covering is a beautiful woman

"For if a woman has long hair, it is a glory to her: for her hair, is given for a covering."
1 Corinthians 11:15

Morning Glory

Early in the morning, under the mist of dew
A blanket of unavailing love spreads over
A whisper so soft and sweet, His glory is everywhere
Can't take everything in what He is revealing to me

Silence so powerful but spoken words I heard
His glory everywhere
As I looked the fog began to push away
Can still see the morning glory; it still appeared

Talking with Him, and He with me
Sharing things that are hidden and deep within
He listens, hears and remembered them no more
His glory is everywhere

Moved closer to embrace His touch
Enjoying every moment as morning fades away
I'll come back tomorrow, and I visit again
Early, under the mist of dew
To meet my Morning Glory oh so sweet

"But thou O Lord, art a shield for me; my glory, and the lifter up of mine head."
Psalm 3:3

Never Alone

I will never leave you nor forsake you
This is what His word says He would do
Fear no evil for I am with thee
Thy rod and thy staff with you I will be

Though a host should encamp around
Stand firm knowing you are on solid ground
Live every day that you have been sent
In God, you can stay confident

You are never alone
The earth is Lord's and thy fullness thereof
Surely goodness and mercy shall follow thee
All the days of your life

Don't fret thyself because of evildoers
You are never alone
Trust in the Lord and do good
You are not alone; God is with thee

You are never alone
Rest and delight thyself in the Lord
Bless the Lord at all times
Because you are never alone

He that dwelleth in the secret place of the Most High, shall abide under the shadow of the
Almighty."

Psalm 91:1

Never Would Have Made It

Never would have made it came the flashback.
Think about it when the devil makes his attacks.
The irony of it all is He dies.
Blood and water poured from His side.

Never would have made it I do realize.
Christ paid the price when for all He died.
The Rugged Cross bore the image of His death.
From the Cross to the grave He was laid to rest.

Never would have made it, but on the third day.
He got up from the grave our debts he would pay.
Forgiveness we can ask when we sin.
Salvation is here for all men.

Never would have made it through my stormy weather.
Try to tell this to all my sisters and brothers.
He is my strength when I need Him most.
Thank God for the in dwelling of the Holy Ghost.

Never would have made it through the lonely hours.
Without His grace and mercy and His Holy Power.
I never would have it.
Lord, without you, I never would have made it.

"For in the time of trouble He shall hide me in his pavilion: in the secret of his tabernacle shall he hide me; he shall set me up upon a rock."

Psalm 27:5

Oh, the Joy that Floods My Soul

I never knew life could be so wonderful
Oh, the joy that flooded my soul
When Jesus came in my heart and made me whole
Oh, the joy that flooded my soul

The guilt and shame He took away
Oh, the joy that flooded my soul
I accept Him as Lord on that special day
Oh, the joy that flooded my soul

The Holy Ghost I could not hide you see
Oh, the joy that flooded my soul
His anointing that came over me
Oh, the joy that flooded my soul

Living and walking in the Master's will
Oh, the joy that flooded my soul
Peace and victory I have still
Oh, the joy that flooded my soul

One day, I will be with Him forever
Oh, the joy that flooded my soul
No more pain and sorrow never
Oh, the joy that flooded my soul

"I will bless the Lord at all times: and His praise shall continually be in my mouth."

Psalm: 34: 1

Promise Me

Promise me, your love will never fade away
Promise me, you're the one I can count on every day
Promise me if I am overcome with fear
Promise me you let me know that you are here

Promise me your love will be gentle and not one that hurts
Promise me you will lift me up and don't make me feel like dirt
Promise me you will be there to hold my hand
Promise me if doubt comes you will let me know I can

Promise me I will be the one you always adore
Promise me you will be there to greet me at the door
Promise me my love you will always embrace
Promise me you will listen and support my case

Promise me when the day comes to a rest
Promise me our love will still be the best
Promise me when the evening dies
Promise me our love will be as a dear prize

Promise me we honor God's word together
Promise me we will obey it and cherish it forever
Promise me our love will be until our days are done
Promise me the love we share will be strong until our race is won

"O Magnify the Lord with me, and let us exalt his name together."

Psalm 34:3

Refuge

He is the potter, and I am the clay
I'll let no one take this away
To my Savior, I will always pray
Under his refuge I will stay

Storm of life can't take me down
Even when false accusers have treated me wrong
To my Savior, I will always pray
Under His refuge I will stay

Troubles of life sometimes great and small
Jesus will be there to free us from them all
To my Savior, I will always pray
Under His refuge I will stay

Oh, what needless pain we sometime bear
When don't we take everything to God in prayer?
To my Savior, I will always pray
Under His refuge I will stay

"God is our refuge and strength, a very present help in trouble."

Psalm 46: 1

Remember Me

Remember me when I am overwhelmed
Remember me when I may cry in front of them
Remember me when my days grow longer
Remember me when for your word I do hunger

Remember me when I'm walking alone
Remember me when all I can do is mourn
Remember me when I can't see my way
Remember me when nothing I can say

Remember me when I am misunderstood
Remember me when I'm doing the best I could
Remember me when the cloud seems to hang low
Remember me when I feel like walking through the door

Remember me when I can't feel your power divine
Remember me when they steal from me what is mine
Remember me when pain is all I feel
Remember me when I have done my best, but did not get a fair deal

Remember me when I am forgiven for sin
Remember me when I am not forgiven by men
Remember me when I try to tell your redemption story
Remember me and I will give you the Glory
Remember me

For he shall give his angels charge over thee, to keep thee in all thy ways.

Psalm 91: 11

Saints Lie Too

Walking around with head held high
Doing just fine and highly favored, they would say
Many wearing a visage pleasing to man
Saints don't lie intentionally because they can

Home in which they live is not protected
Wives praying and doing everything, trying to make it
Her love for God she holds dear inside
Walking around with things she tries to hide

Saints lie this is true
Some don't talk, but you can see the clue
Trying hard, she will give you a smile
Knowing this is just for a little while

To church, both of them go each week
She hides the pain while God she seeks
Saints lie to protect the one they love in office each year
Lord knows the pain is sometimes hard to bear

Saints don't lie intentionally
Hoping things would change eventuality
Greeting each other in church they will do this
At home, wives don't even get one little kiss

Saints don't lie because they can
Just trying to show a good face to man
God forgive me they often cry
Pressing on to that mention in the sky

"Give ear to my prayer, o God; and hide not thyself from my supplication."

Psalm: 55: 1

Silent

Silent instead of the spoken word
Sometime things need to be heard
Won't let it drive me insane
Asked God to move the hurt and pain

Spoken words, they are very few
What's on the mind, I don't have a clue
It's like walking slowly toward a ledge
Being hit by a great big steel wedge

Silent instead of the spoken word
Sometimes things need to be heard
Won't let it rob me of my dignity
I know communication is the key

Silent that is so strong you can't say nay
To know what you are thinking, speaking is the way
Silent instead of the spoken word
Sometimes things need to be heard

"He restoreth my soul: he leadeth me in the paths of righteousness for his Name's sake.
Psalm: 23:

Single

Black, single, and dreads that hang down her back
Pain, stain, and enduring many attacks
Chosen by God to witness to the nation
The battle came from the enemy to test her patience

Many sleepless nights the pain kept her awake
The birthing is hard and long as she awaits daybreak
Daybreak comes, she is renewed again
Lord, strengthen me and take away this pain

A mother of one, the father is not there
The struggles of life and the disappointment she had to bear
It won't stop her; the devil is a liar
Each day the Holy Spirit takes her higher

Black, single, and pretty as a peach
Call by God to witness and teach
Pain, stain, and enduring many attacks
Tears, heartbreaks, and many times depressed
Did not last, it was only a test

Arms stretch out to help everyone
Even though many times taking from her son
The joy she gets when she helps others
Gave her last to help her sisters and brothers

Single don't mean there is something wrong
She will tell you when she sings her songs
When she sings, it is not the tone but the words
In the words her story can be heard

Tall, strong, and pretty as a peach
It's the God in me, to others she tries to teach
Blessed by God this is no whisper
The single lady's name is Kristle

"I can do all things through Christ which strengthen me."

Philippians 4: 1

Sister

(Written especially for my sister, Rebecca who is in a Nursing Home in North Augusta 2015)

Sister, I wish you could get out of bed, the things you could see.
Without help, I guess this is where you will be.
Heading to see you driving along in my car.
Wondering why you had to move so far.
A better place, a team who knows how to take care of you.
Remember you not alone, Jesus promise to be there too.

Traveling down the road, a song I would sing and a prayer I would pray.
Lord, bless my sister and keep her day by day.
Be encouraged my sister and hold on with all of your might.
Your family holds you in their hearts oh so very tight.

If the pain gets too hard to bear, just whisper a little prayer.
You not alone, Jesus will always be near.
Long days and sleepless nights you had some.
Be strong, and patient; tell yourself my healing will come.
Weeping only endures for a night.
In the morning, everything will be alright.

Teased

Teased about how you may look
Cruel things, yes, you may have took
Sometimes the teasing may have been bad
Love to give was all you had

Tried to give a little smile
Even if it was just for a little while
Teasing is cruel and with disrespect
The victims still try to give respect

The teasing even though breaks your heart
Never let teasing tear you apart
Don't let teasing get to you; Jesus is a friend that will always stay true
Take the teaser to Jesus, he already knows who

Let me share some Black History
Things we endured even when they declared we were free
Be proud to know the stand our ancestors took
Even though you won't find it all in the history book

Our skin color others may laugh at
A protection in the hot sun many have sat
Know your roots and teasing won't take a toll on you
Don't stop loving, let them see the good you can still do

Oh, the thanks and praise you should give unto thee
He was the one that set us free
When you are teased because the color of your skin
It is not your looks but what lies within

When you are teased know you are a child of the King
Joy and happiness He will bring
Remember what was done to Him on the cross
Even when He was dying so we won't be lost

The Backyard Garden

The backyard garden is a place where I often meet
Alone many times, but it is still so sweet
Early morning, I meet it in prayer
A place that I love, so very dear

The garden is a friend you can visit anytime
The birds the bees and all in beautiful chimes
Flowers, flowers everywhere
A garden of roses all planted in pairs

The garden is very special and unique
Watch it transforms and changes every week
The amazing colors remind you that spring is coming soon
Listen closely to the birds, all humming a special tune

The garden embraces many celebrations
Use it for your picnics and family vacations
Taking pictures, playing and having fun
Enjoying life in the morning and midday sun

The backyard garden is a place I often meet
Lone many times, but it is still so sweet
Trees, flowers, a pond even pictures on the wall
The joy I find just digging in the soil

"The earth is the Lord's, and the fullness thereof."

Psalm: 24:1

The Doctor Within

Went to the Doc for a follow up, you see
The doc was nice and sweet as he could be
Signed in and then sat down
People were there from all around town

Called me back oh so quick
Thought I'll be out in just a tick
In the small room I kept hearing this cough
While I listen to this voice oh so soft

Finally, heard a voice next door
Maybe the doc, I looked even more
The delay was not mines, nor the doc's
It was from above; the delay was already on the clock

I looked through the window, saw trees with no leaves stand still
A blind open and lying on the windowsill
The small room I remember so well that day
About the delay, I had nothing to say

The **Doctor within** began to speak
I listen quietly and stayed humble and meek
Looking at the floor, each tile had the same square
In a corner was a small black chair

The stool where the doc sits was bare
The **Doctor within** let me know He was still there
Step off the table and got my pen and began to write
The **Doctor within** let me know everything was alright

Comfort began to fill the air
Just knowing the **Doctor** was still there
I did not know what the doc would say
My trust in God, I continue to pray

Finally, the door opened, and the doc came in
His nurse followed with a pad and pen
See you back in six months he said
I asked him about the test he had read

No changes since you were here last
Talking about the appointment in months past
The **Doctor Within** never diminished
Felt His present from start to finish

"He that dwelleth in the secret place of the most high shall abide under the shadow of the Almighty. I will say of the Lord He is m y refuge and my fortress: my God; in him will I trust."

Psalm: 91: 1-2

The Stairs

(This poem is a Vision I saw of our Dear Beloved Bishop William L. Bonner, gone but not forgotten)

It was in a meeting one night
The lights were oh so bright
People I knew were there
Some in rows and others sat in chairs

The stairs were tall and steep
They stretched so long and were so deep
Starting from the bottom, all the way to the top
Had to climb and could not stop

One foot on the stairs, I began to climb
Felt I didn't have a lot of time
The meeting I left behind was in high gear
Kept climbing, the top was drawing near

Finally, the flight to the top was all done
An open door I came upon
Went inside took a peep
Things that were so dear I wanted to keep

Books were everywhere.
The Genius of the man I declare
His clothes and robes fold so neatly on chairs
So overwhelmed I wanted to burst into tears

I got a glimpse of this vessel that was so dear
The anointed in the room seemed everywhere
The things left behind for me to see
Show me what kind of man was he

The stairs that led me to that place
From there he taught many, God's Amazing Grace
Now he is gone to his home above
Left behind his children, the ones he truly loved

The stairs that I climb were in a dream
Everything I saw was all so real it seems
We will one day meet in that sweet by and by,
In our heavenly home beyond the sky

"Finally, my brethren, be strong in the Lord, and in the power of his might.
Put on the whole armor of God that you may be able to stand against the wiles of the devil."

Ephesians 6:10-11

Understand

Understand when I say I love you
Understand when I say my love is true
Understand when I say I need a hug
Understand when I am not feeling well or have a bug

Understand when I want to talk
Understand when I just want to take a walk
Understand when I say we need to pray
Understand when I say Jesus is the only way

Understand when I want to be romanced
Understand when I say I want to dance
Understand when I say you are the only one
Understand when I say it's your love or none

Understand when I say I just want to smell the flower
Understand when I say I am wet from the rain shower
Understand when I am in the shower and the water is running down
Understand oh how I which I would hear a beautiful song

Understand when in the stillness of the night
Understand I want you to hold me tight
Understand when we walk through the door
Our love for each other, everyone will know

"Trust in the Lord with all thine heart; and lean not unto thine own understanding. I all thy ways acknowledge him, and he shall direct thy paths".

Provide: 3: 5-6

Vision On The Wall

Vision on the wall
A man that stands so tall
The Holy Christ He was there
The power of God everywhere

The vision on the wall
A man that stands so tall
He was the one who died on the cross
Man sins he carried, so we won't be lost

Vision on the wall
A man that stands so tall
Sweat and agony cover his face
On the cross he hanged to plead our case

Vision on the wall
A man that stands so tall
It was Jesus, the one who died for you and me
In heaven with Him, one day we will be

Vision on the wall
A man that stands so tall
The power of his Holy Trinity
Reminding us of life eternity

"I press toward the mark for the prize of the high calling of God in Christ Jesus."

Philippians: 3:14

Where Do I Go From Here?

Where do I go from here?
A part of my daily prayer
Many years he has kept me
The honor and glory I give to thee

A new phase of life I enter this day
God is good, this I must say
My purpose, my destiny I continue to seek
Every month, every day, and every week

The pain of labor very hard
I must keep His holy charge
After the birthing the joy it brings
Hallelujah to our King

Quietly listening to God's holy voice
Waiting, waiting before I make my choice
Sometimes days oh seem like nights
But I can feel His hands holding me tight

Cheer up my child and lift your head
Oh, this day I clearly heard Him when He said
You are never alone, remember that song?
Felt little better, but still ponder what I've done wrong

Where do I go from here, I must decide
Release, release the hurt from inside
Struggle to find a new path for me
Strengthen me Lord so I'll be
Out of the prison Lord and be free
And I'll go from here!

"For everyone that asketh, receiveth and he that seeketh findeth and to him that knocketh it shall be opened."

Mathew 7: 8

Where Would I Go?

Where would I go, is the demon that holds us back
So we stay and take all the cruel attacks
Too afraid to make the move out of there
We stay and take it from someone who don't even care

Name calling, and to my body, even hits
She stays right there and with his demand she will sit
All the harsh words and the cursing
It is me; she says as things worsen

Where would I go, runs through her mind
The things she is called are never kind
God gave the woman to man as a help meet
Not someone for man to scorn or beat

Ladies look in the mirror and what do you see?
Are you the woman God called you to be?
Stay strong and don't be afraid to take your leap
Don't be saddened over the things he told you he will keep

Where would I go?
Know that God will provide.
This is America, the home of freedom and pride
Don't let this demon destroy you anymore
Have the courage and asked God, is this the time for me to walk out of this door

"And the Lord God said, it is not good that the man should be alone; I will make him and help meet for him".

Genesis: 2:18

WHO AM I?

I AM A WOMAN

TAKEN FROM THE RIB OF THE MAN.

CREATED BY GOD'S ALMIGHTY HANDS.

STRONG AND HUMBLE THERE SHE STANDS.

WILLING TO HELP WHERE EVER SHE CAN.

A HELP MEET, WITHOUT A DOUBT.

CARING AND LOVING, THAT'S WHAT SHE IS ALL ABOUT.

GOD GAVE MAN THE WOMAN AT CREATION.

OH WHAT A WONDERFUL REVELATION.

SHE TRUST GOD IN EVERY WAY.

SHE PRAYS TO HIM EVERYDAY.

"I AM A WOMAN."

Struggles, when they come can sometimes separate people from their God, but never God from His People. God has always been faithful. He has always kept His Promises. Even when it feels like we are walking *"through the valley of the shadow of death, fear no Evil"*, for God is with us.

In the pages of this book, my prayer is that it will encourage, empower, and fuel your faith. I am a Living Witness that no matter what you may encounter or may have to go through; God will be there for you. Your Struggles are not isolated from God. He knows and sees all things. He knows all about our Struggles.

His word says we are more than a Conqueror. Jesus has been my strength, my everything. When I needed him the Most, He was there for me. Let Him be there for you. When struggles comes don't let it take your Joy. Don't let it turn your love away from God. Don't let it defeat you. Let your experiences bring you closer to God.

-Rachael B. Jenkins

Reflection Notes

Made in the USA
Columbia, SC
24 June 2021

40526004R00036